T0145061

My First Brain Book

Written and Illustrated
by Dr. Megan Finneran

Copyright © 2023 Dr. Megan Finneran.

All rights reserved. No part of this book may be used or reproduced by any means, graphic, electronic, or mechanical, including photocopying, recording, taping or by any information storage retrieval system without the written permission of the author except in the case of brief quotations embodied in critical articles and reviews.

Archway Publishing books may be ordered through booksellers or by contacting:

Archway Publishing
1663 Liberty Drive
Bloomington, IN 47403
www.archwaypublishing.com
844-669-3957

Because of the dynamic nature of the Internet, any web addresses or links contained in this book may have changed since publication and may no longer be valid. The views expressed in this work are solely those of the author and do not necessarily reflect the views of the publisher, and the publisher hereby disclaims any responsibility for them.

Any people depicted in stock imagery provided by Getty Images are models, and such images are being used for illustrative purposes only.
Certain stock imagery © Getty Images.

ISBN: 978-1-6657-4785-1 (sc)
ISBN: 978-1-6657-4786-8 (hc)
ISBN: 978-1-6657-4787-5 (e)

Library of Congress Control Number: 2023914261

Print information available on the last page.

Archway Publishing rev. date: 07/29/2023

To my wonderful mom, Kate, the master of the rhyme.
Whose words of encouragement to dream big will be with
me for all of time.

And to amore mio, Emilio, my husband and teacher too.
I cannot imagine this book (or life!) without you.

Welcome to the brain!
Do you know all it can do?

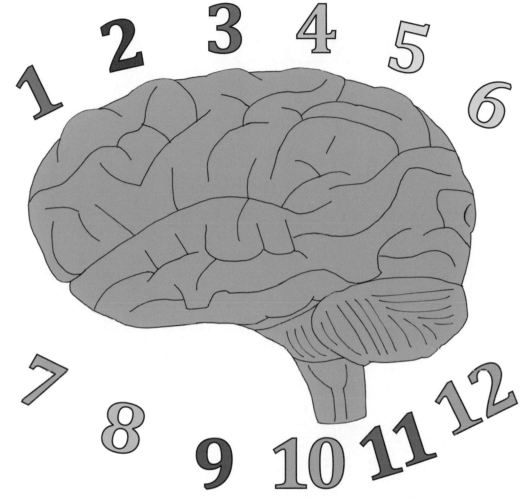

Today we are learning about the twelve cranial nerves and how they help make you YOU.

Sniff, sniff, sniff...

what do you smell?

Cranial nerve ONE, olfactory, helps your nose to tell.

What color is that?
What animal is there in the tree?

2

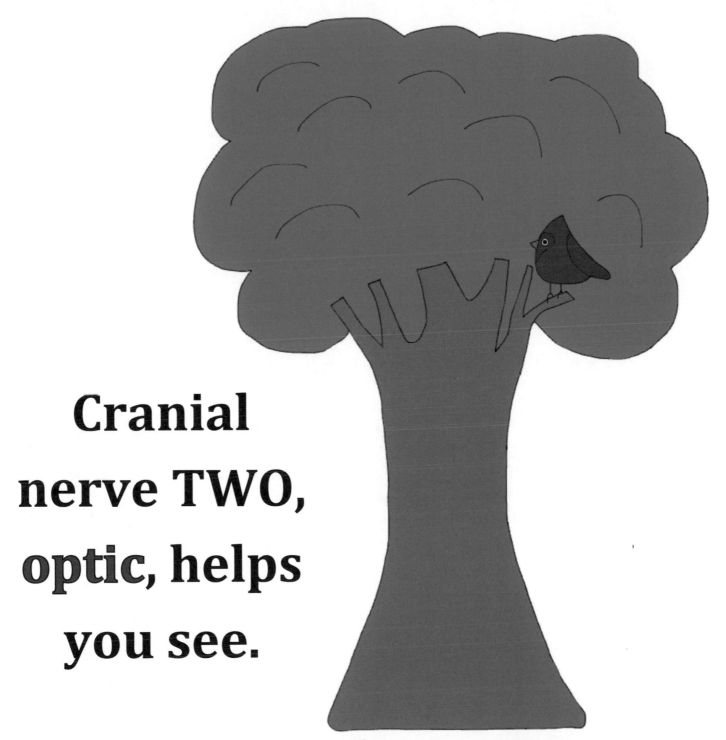

Cranial nerve TWO, optic, helps you see.

Open your
eyes big!
Look at
the
ground
and the
sky.

3

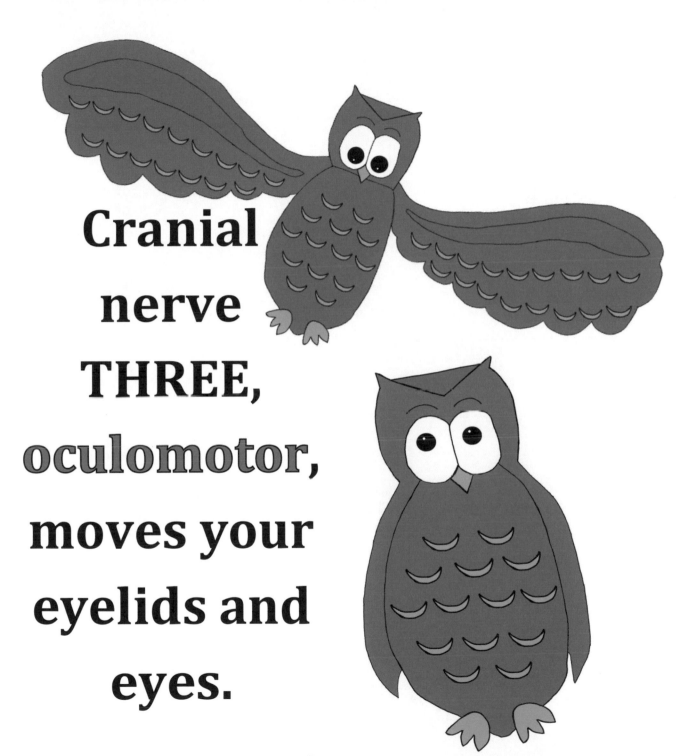

Cranial nerve THREE, oculomotor, moves your eyelids and eyes.

4

Look down at the floor, then look side to side.

Cranial nerve FOUR, trochlear, gives your eyes that ride.

Rub your nose on a soft fluffy spot.

Cranial nerve FIVE, trigeminal, **helps your face feel if something is touching or not.**

Follow the line!
From left to right and back.

6

Cranial nerve SIX, abducens, helps your eyes track.

Close your eyes tight,

puff out your cheeks.

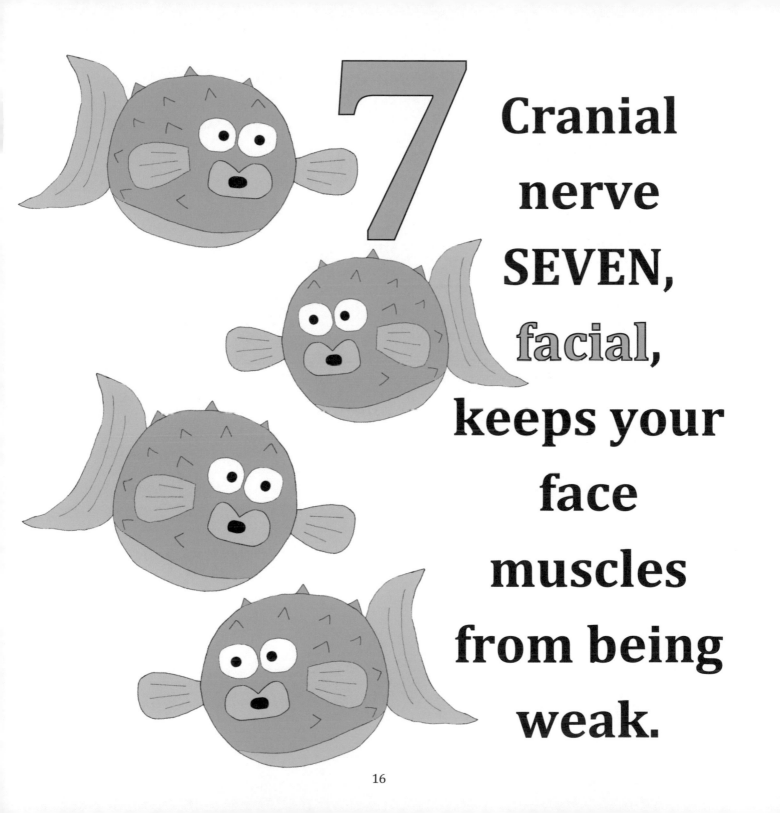

Cranial nerve SEVEN, facial, keeps your face muscles from being weak.

Clap your hands! Can you hear that sound?

Cranial nerve EIGHT, vestibulocochlear, helps you hear all around.

What is your favorite food? Think of how it tastes.

9

Cranial nerve NINE, glossopharyngeal, helps you taste the yummy things on your plate.

Open your mouth wide and say AHHHHHHHHHHH - hold it!

Cranial nerve TEN, vagus, helps you swallow your spit.

Shrug your shoulders up,

tilt your head left and right.

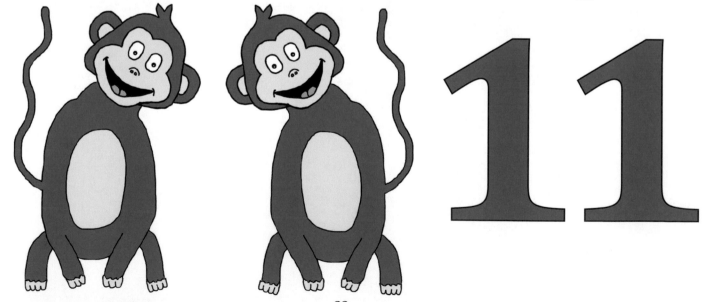

11

Cranial nerve ELEVEN, spinal accessory, keeps your neck muscles tight.

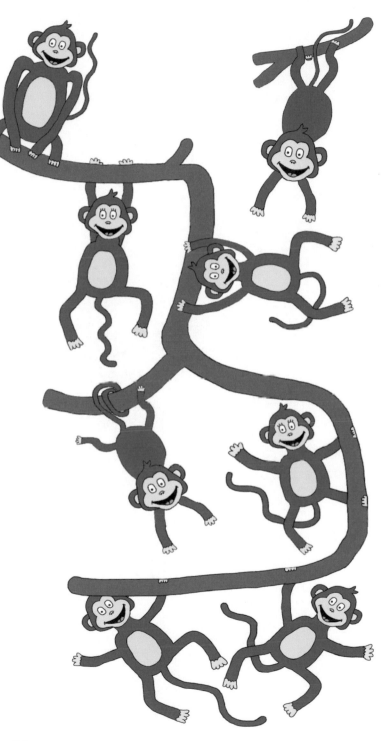

Wiggle your tongue. Stick it out all the way!

Cranial nerve TWELVE, glossopharyngeal, helps your tongue stray.

Thanks for joining for the fun!

Did you learn a lot today?

1 2 3 4 5 6
7 8 9 10 1112

Now you know about your amazing brain and all its powers you can display.

Printed in the United States
by Baker & Taylor Publisher Services